YOUR SOCIAL PRACTICE

HOW SOCIAL MEDIA MARKETING
TRANSFORMS & GROWS DENTAL PRACTICES

—

JACK HADLEY

TABLE OF CONTENTS

—

PREFACE

—

In early 2012 I was contacted by the MBA Marketing Curriculum Chairman, Glenn Christensen, at Brigham Young University's Marriott School of Management. At that time I was teaching advertising as an adjunct professor in the undergrad program at BYU. Glenn knew that I had founded a dental social media marketing company, and that significant portions of the content I was teaching in my classes focused on social media.

BYU's MBA program didn't yet offer digital marketing classes—in fact, there were only a couple of MBA programs in the country that had begun including such classes in their curriculums. Glenn asked me if I would be willing to help them develop a digital marketing track and then teach the Social Media Marketing class in that track. I agreed, and doing so has been a remarkably rewarding experience.

There's an important reason why this experience in academia is pertinent to this book's purpose.

In preparing new materials for the students in my MBA class each year, I spend a lot of time researching and reviewing social media marketing case studies, including strategies and tactics utilized by both large enterprise brands and small companies and organizations. And while the objectives are different for businesses of various types and sizes, I've become convinced that small, relationship-based businesses—e.g. dental and dental specialty practices—benefit from social media marketing (when it's understood and effectively implemented) more than any other business type.

Large brands and organizations may have bigger budgets and greater resources. But dollar-for-dollar and minute-for-minute invested, relationship-based businesses can focus on social media marketing's core benefit—that is, leveraging one-to-one relationships.

Think about it! Very few businesses enjoy the privilege of having customers (or patients) walk through their door at least a couple of times each year and sit with them face to face, knee to knee, and even hand to mouth! These are intimate, personal connections. Perhaps hairdressers and personal trainers enjoy similar relationships with their clients, but this business structure is rare. And while I understand why some critics label social media activity "faux intimacy," in the case of dental practices, its physicality makes it real. It makes it genuine. It makes it human.

Effective dental social media marketing doesn't start online—it starts inside the practice. If your practice's social media feels faux, you're doing something wrong.

In my early twenties, I was fascinated by a wave of new companies driving personal time management concepts. When Hyrum W. Smith founded the Franklin Quest Company and started printing huge 7-ring Franklin Day Planners around 1982, I was among the first to enroll in his earliest personal time management courses centered around the utilization of those incredibly bulky day planners! Franklin Quest eventually merged with Stephen R. Covey's Covey Leadership Center to form the company Franklin Covey.

As a budding entrepreneur, this training was life-changing for me! I enthusiastically committed one of Hyrum's adages to memory—a maxim that still comes to my mind nearly every day. "When your daily activities are in harmony with your highest priorities, you have a credible claim to inner peace."

I've modified Hyrum's adage with the hope that you'll commit my adaptation to memory; "When your social media activities are in harmony with your practice values and business objectives, you have a credible claim to transformation and growth."

"Transformation and growth," you ask? Read on!

WITH GRATITUDE

First and foremost, thanks to our tens of thousands of My Social Practice fans, followers and valued clients. We're honored and humbled by the love you show our company. We appreciate you more than you could know. Thanks for subscribing to our content. Thanks for continuing to teach me. Thanks for supporting our business.

Second, thanks to our My Social Practice team members. Your enthusiasm and empathy for our clients is inspiring. We're proud of you.

Third, thanks to Christine Hill for helping me write this book! We miss having you as a writer at My Social Practice. Thank you for reining me in and for using your gifts to get this book written.

Fourth, thank you, Mollie Bohannon, for the great job you did designing the book. Beautifully done. We miss you too!

Fifth, thanks to my three business partners, Seth, Adrian and Blake, who bring 100 percent of their talents and effort to the table each day to grow and sustain our business. And thanks to Rob (our former partner who has gone on to bigger things) for believing in My Social Practice and helping it grow during its far-more-dubious, formative years.

And finally, thanks to my amazing wife and crazy-talented kids for putting up with their often knuckleheaded husband and father who takes on far more projects than he should.

INTRODUCTION

—

When you're in an airliner, the world looks very different from 10,000 feet. Have you ever considered a 10,000-foot view of your dental practice? When you step back and think about it, what does your practice really offer? What kind of business would you have if you removed dentistry altogether? Sound crazy? Research suggests that only 15 percent of a practice's success is dependent on the dentist's clinical expertise.

Flourishing dental practices don't focus on what they make (dentistry), but instead, focus on what they make possible—and on the experience of being a patient in their practice.

Health. Confidence. Peace of mind. Community. Smart practices' values and business objectives extend well beyond funds, fillings and flossing. Your effective marketing strategies must do the same. But before we start talking about dental social media marketing, let's paint a picture of what the end goal might look like.

What type of patients do you want? Keepers? You can decide! Be bold about it. Not cocky, but confident. Believe it or not, social media marketing can single-handedly give you that choice.

Flourishing practices constantly remind themselves of the *kinds* of new patients they want to bring through their door and then retain—not just the *number* of new patients they want to bring through that door. Then, they align their social media marketing activities in such a way as to attract and retain those kinds of patients. Of course, patience is a must while cultivating this base of patients. It doesn't happen overnight, but it's still a choice you can make.

Effective social media marketing serves "higher purposes" in addition to putting derrières in chairs. It can nurture a specific mindset about doing business. Through words, actions, and visuals, social media marketing reinforces that what you're doing each day matters, in many different ways.

Social media activity can become the outward-facing manifestation of an inward-facing practice culture of appreciation and gratitude. It can not only strengthen patient relationships and grow your business, but it can positively impact you and your team members in very personal ways. It can impact the communities you serve.

There are three chapters in this book. Here's why...

As a former copywriter, ad agency creative director and epiphany catalyst I've developed hundreds of message architectures over the years. As such, I've relied heavily on certain tactics that bring messaging clarity to marketing projects.

I've used one of these tactics to help create the content for this book. It's often referred to as "The Six Ws," although it's actually five Ws and one H: who, why, when, where, what and how. Three of those six are the most foundational and they correspond to this book's three chapters. Chapter one, "Practices Flourish Through Transformation & Growth" is the why. Chapter two, "The Six Principles of Effective

Dental Social Media Marketing" is the what. And chapter three, "The 3-Part Strategy" is the how.

Never before in the history of dental marketing has a practice really been able to own its story. Traditionally, you relied on others to convey little slivers of your story. An ad agency printed and snail-mailed postcards for you, and the yellow pages rep designed your new half-page ad. Businesses didn't do their marketing. It was left to the "professionals."

Today, social media marketing can make telling your story your opportunity. Doing so—and embracing the process itself—can bring a sense of business clarity and peace of mind that you've never experienced before, knowing that you're in control. Owning your story is empowering, and it doesn't need to consume you or take a lot of your precious time.

Social media can not only grow your practice, but it can also **positively impact you** in very personal ways.

Also, it doesn't matter if you're a general dentist or specialist. Why? Because once you've read this book you'll understand why effective dental social media marketing is no more about "selling dentistry" than it is about selling endodontics, periodontics, orthodontics or any other specialty service. It's about other things.

This book is about those other things. This book is about mindset, not tools. This book is about rejecting scarcity mentality. This book is about starting something with the humility that comes in being unsure, yet sensing the value of what it will become. This book is about the sustained effectiveness of being human in your dental marketing.

This book is about transformation and growth for your flourishing practice—facilitated through effective social media marketing. For dental professionals with open minds and open hearts, this book will be about much more than marketing. And if you've read this far, I'm probably talking about you.

01

CHAPTER ONE
Practices Flourish Through Transformation & Growth

—

Social media marketing is about so much more than marketing. When understood and embraced, it not only grows a practice, it transforms it. Social media marketing requires practices to do some things, create some things, prioritize some things and stand for some things. It requires believing that what you do in your practice matters. Social media marketing is about humility, giving, and taking action. Smart practices today view social media marketing as a catalyst for transformation and growth.

I'm a big Peter Drucker fan. He was a business consultant and thought leader who many considered a founder of modern business success. He said, "A business has only one valid purpose: to create a customer. And if the purpose of a business is to create a customer, then that business only has two functions—innovation and marketing. Innovation and marketing produce results. All the rest are costs. Innovation produces the product and marketing tells the stories that sell the product."

I've modified Peter's quote and made it specific to dental marketing. Here's my edited version:

"A practice has only one valid purpose: to create a patient. And if the purpose of a practice is to create a patient, then that practice only has two functions—innovation and marketing. Innovation produces clinical expertise and management effectiveness. Marketing tells the stories that fuel growth."

Peter Drucker's hypothesis (along with my edits) provides a framework that creates context for our social media marketing discussion.

Practices only have **two functions**:
1. innovation, and
2. marketing

Practices only have **three ingredients**:
1. clinical expertise,
2. management effectiveness, and
3. growth

When we match up the two functions with the three ingredients we're left with a remarkably simple way to view the business of running a practice. Doing so also brings clarity to the important role of marketing and growth.

CRUCIAL PRACTICE **FUNCTIONS**	CRUCIAL PRACTICE **INGREDIENTS**
INNOVATION	**CLINICAL EXPERTISE**
	MANAGEMENT EFFECTIVENESS
MARKETING	**GROWTH**

While I'm certainly not discounting the importance of clinical expertise and management effectiveness, this book is about growth.

In this book's preface, I referenced practice values, business objectives, and practice culture. I know they vary from practice to practice. What's "ownable" about yours? It's important to consider them as you read this book because they become the fodder for the stories that attract and retain patients. Social media marketing helps us become better storytellers.

Right up front, I'm going to make two bold, broad assertions. First, you want your practice to flourish. Second, your practice will flourish through the transformation and growth that effective social media marketing provides.

CHARACTERISTICS OF FLOURISHING PRACTICES

Consider a flourishing practice the same way you would consider a flourishing plant. You can quickly boost a plant's growth using chemicals. It's certainly a way to spike volume. However, long-term, sustained organic growth is preferable, which happens naturally when a plant is happy, healthy, and cared for.

- Flourishing practices treat people, not teeth.

- Flourishing practices deeply value patient relationships.

- Flourishing practices change patients' lives and team members' lives.

- Flourishing practices change people's lives who are connected to the practice through community.

- Flourishing practices are highly profit-able but never consumed by the primary premise of making money. Making money is a by-product of the things flourishing practices do each day with purpose.

- Flourishing practices are places where gratitude not only abounds, but is expressed through action.

- Flourishing practices are constantly transforming, which fuels sustained growth.

This flourishing plant analogy may seem out of place, coming from a marketer. Typically, when people think about marketing they ARE, in fact, thinking about quickly boosting growth using chem-icals (like advertising). But social media marketing ("new" marketing) is much different than traditional marketing and advertising. Focusing on social media marketing as the means for becoming a flourishing practice, starts inside the practice, then naturally radiates out.

Creating a flourishing practice isn't about slapping on a new coat of paint. It's not about a new logo or a new website. It's not about using social media for shock value, to be outrageous, or to garner attention merely for the sake of attention. It's about the long-term, sustained organic growth that happens naturally when a practice is passionate about telling the stories that attract and retain patients.

SUSTAINED TRANSFORMATION FUELS SUSTAINED GROWTH

You may be thinking, "Jack, I thought this was a marketing book. I thought you were just going to give us the secret formula for using social media to get new patients. What do you mean by 'transformation'? What are we transforming from? What are we transforming to?" Thanks for asking.

Let's dive in by allowing me to ask you a question. Do your current patients love you? They might like you for certain baseline things: a gentle touch during cleanings, perhaps, or how convenient your location is to their home? Maybe they like you for the "lifetime free whitening" perk you enticed them with to become a new patient. But those things will never be the reasons patients love you. They will never be reasons that inspire passion within them to tell their friends, extended family members and coworkers about you. They'll never be reasons why they remain patients and happily drive an hour for their appointments long after they've moved to a neighboring city. They'll never be reasons why they readily accept the optional treatment recommendations you make.

Do your team members love being at work? Are they proud of what they do each day? Are they energized (even giddy at times) when they participate in helping promote the stories that define your practice?

When we talk about marketing and telling your practice's story we usually think about the outward-

Social media activity can become the

OUTWARD-FACING EXPRESSIONS

OF INWARD-FACING VALUES.

facing messages first, and the inward-facing ones second. What are these inward-facing messages? How can they invoke contagious passion? When you and your team feel more fulfilled by what you do each day, your patients feel it too. Social media can help with that. A lot.

Sure, I understand. Many times the things we do each day don't seem very interesting or significant. Most days feel pretty routine. It's that way in all businesses. Not every patient who walks through your door is a delight. Not every team member is easy to inspire. The challenge in embracing effective social media marketing is in rising above these things and seeing the end goal through the fog. Over and over again I see practices that energize their team and their patients through effective social media activity—by telling their practice's story with passion.

So, what are we using social media marketing to transform to and from? Here are a few things...

- From focusing on what you make (dentistry) to focusing on what you make possible.

- From trying to be interesting, to being interested.
- From being angry with patients who miss appointments to cultivating the loyalty that prevents it.
- From gut-wrenching doubt about your marketing spend to peace of mind.
- From trying to steal the other guy's piece of the pie to making the pie bigger.
- From hunting for new patients to helping new patients find you.
- From abdicating your practice's story to owning it and confidently telling it.
- From selling to permission-based marketing.
- From trying to demand attention to actually giving people reasons to pay attention, and to care.
- From marketing charlatan babble to simple marketing principles and welcomed clarity.
- From viewing marketing as a burden to actually enjoying it.
- From dentistry as a commodity to the experience of being your patient.

- From scarcity mentality to abundance mentality.
- From charitable activity to charitable activity that's noticed and grows your practice. (Hey, it's OK! As long as you're FIRST doing things for the right reason!)
- From dependence on search engine gurus to helping steer your own digital footprint.
- From marketing driven by fear to marketing confidence that people feel.
- From online irrelevance to relevance.
- From old school thinking to "new marketing's" effectiveness.

Transformation isn't an overnight process. It's ongoing and must be sustained. It's not a quick fix, and it's certainly not just about surface changes. Achieving success will undoubtedly take longer that you would like it to. And don't forget... This transformation is a journey, not a destination. You'll actually never be finished. That's a good thing, by the way.

Think about the journey the way you might think about providing a smile makeover. Let's say that

Don't focus on what you **make**.

Focus on what you **make possible.**

one day a patient comes to you asking for a smile makeover. In her head, she's only thinking about the aesthetics. She wants to look better! However, you know that a remarkable smile makeover isn't just about aesthetics. It's also about optimal function, balance and health. You know that the most engaging smiles are always those that radiate confidence and health, as well as beauty. Style follows function.

This may require a longer process than your patient initially imagined, or a different aesthetic approach than the one she envisioned. But you're confident that when she sees the beautiful, sustainable end result you've provided she'll be ecstatic about the transformation. In the same way, the transformation we're talking about for your practice must be based on the sustainable, long-term result. And that takes time. The difference here is that this patient's smile makeover journey will conclude. Marketing doesn't.

Prior to having these powerful digital tools at our fingertips, it was nearly impossible to easily and affordably demonstrate expressions of commitment, or to communicate your practice values to patients and prospective new patients. What could your practice become if every patient, team member, and prospective new patient was touched by the constantly-renewed passion that you can express through social media activity? It's a great time to be marketing your dental practice.

HOW PRACTICES GROW

Practices grow in four ways:

1. acquiring new patients,

2. greater patient retention,

3. increased patient spend, and

4. cost savings

We won't be talking about #4, cost savings, in this book because that's primarily a management discussion, not a marketing discussion. But the first three growth components can be tightly tied to your social media marketing efforts.

1. NEW PATIENTS

Often there are two important things that patients look at when making a decision about a new dentist. They are location and insurance. I certainly don't mean to downplay that reality.

However, this fact doesn't pertain to our marketing discussion. These are practice profile and practice management concerns. Deciding where to locate your practice, and whether or not to accept insurance are decisions you've either already made or decisions that you're working to make with a consultant or other trusted resource.

And although practice location and insurance acceptance are pragmatic considerations in prospective new patient decision making, a recent Futuredontics survey entitled "The Top 5 Reasons Patients Choose a Dentist" found that one out of three patients base their decision on the practice's online reputation. In fact, 86 percent of respondents said they're willing to pay more to become patients at a practice with higher ratings and reviews.

In this book's introduction, I asked you, "What kind of new patients do you want?" Insurance-driven and location-driven patients are a gimme. They are what they are. Stop thinking about them. Your office is located where it's located. You already made that decision. And, you either accept insurance or you don't.

Now, of course we still want these location-driven and insurance-driven patients to enjoy a remarkable experience being your patient. Every person who becomes your patient is super important, no matter how he or she got there. But this section of the book is specific to attracting the new patients we really want! The keepers!

Social media marketing helps you **attract** the kind of patients you want.

Effective new patient, social media marketing efforts are focused on acquiring keepers in three important ways:

ONLINE CONVERSATIONS WITH TRUSTED CONNECTIONS

Word-of-mouth referrals have always been, and will likely remain the best source for new patients you'll consider keepers. 82 percent of prospective new patients ask the people they're connected to for recommendations, and in an increasingly plugged-in, digital-centric world, most of these conversations are happening online.

Recommendations from your patients on social media channels and review sites lead to easier and more effective new-patient conversions.

APPROACHABILITY

People like doing business with people they know, like, and trust. We know how apprehensive and fearful some people are when it comes to seeing a dentist. The familiarity that can come through the informality of your social media efforts can absolutely tip the scales in your favor. You're able to create personable impressions and/or connections with prospective new patients online long before they walk through your door. This can really help patients who may be paralyzed by decision-making fear in choosing a dentist.

PERCEPTIONS AND TRANSFERENCE

Being digitally present, and participating online, establishes a number of things in prospective new patients' minds. First, it shows that you're listening, that you're approachable, that you're tuned in to patient service. Second, it demonstrates that you're transparent, honest and straightforward. You're not like the wizard from The Wizard of Oz who's hiding behind your website curtain! And third, it suggests that you're a technologically-savvy practice which implies that you're also likely to be technologically advanced when it comes to the services you provide, the materials you use, the recommendations you make, and the CE you attend! The perception becomes that you are a modern, progressive practice.

2. RETAINING EXISTING PATIENTS

Each patient you retain is a patient you don't have to replace. It's simple math. Yet the vast majority of dental marketing companies ONLY scream, "New patients! New patients! New patients!" Why? Follow the money.

Conditioning dentists by keeping them in a constant, frenzied panic about finding new patients sustains their business models. They potentially make less money if you start retaining more patients, right? Treating dental professionals like Pavlov's dogs is insulting, frankly.

When it comes to patient retention, effective social media marketing decreases attrition through three important strategies:

STRENGTHENED RELATIONSHIPS

Why do patients leave practices? The vast majority don't leave because they move, die, or because they don't like you anymore. Then why? Studies show that nearly 70 percent of patients who leave a practice do so because of the practice's indifference. Yes, indifference! They don't believe that it will make any difference to you, one way or the other, if they continue being your patient.

That's sad, isn't it?! Especially for an intimate, relationship-based business! They simply don't think anyone will even notice if they leave.

So much of effective dental social media marketing revolves around showing appreciation for, and sustaining these existing, valued relationships. Even a faithful patient who visits your practice

Nearly 70% of patients who leave a practice
do so because of the practice's **indifference.**

every six months can merely have a "polite acquain-tanceship" with your team members until given the opportunity to know them better. Instead of only touching base twice a year, you can use various social media marketing efforts to digitally connect with your patients monthly, weekly and occasionally, even daily! When done thoughtfully, this absolutely strengthens these relationships.

In turn, this becomes reciprocal. When your practice shows more appreciation for patients, those patients will notice and appreciate you more as well. Patients become more personally invested in the experience of being your valued patient.

VALUABLE CONVERSATIONS

Patients are more likely to stay with a practice when they feel like their voice is heard and their needs are met. Are you using social media to invite feedback from your patients?

Social media marketing isn't about lecturing. You don't use an authoritative voice with a loudspeaker. It's about conversations. It's about helping you discover what your patients need and how they're feeling about your practice.

Humans are funny this way. They really like being heard. They appreciate conversations. Then, social media hands you the blessing of being able to easily and effectively respond. Don't forget that social media conversations are meant as much for the hundreds of outsiders who will read them later as they are for the specific people you're responding to. And obviously, there are important patient privacy considerations you must be sensitive to, but that's a discussion for another day.

Use social media to **remind** patients why they chose you.

CONTINUED AFFIRMATION

Patients don't spend nearly as much time thinking about why they should love you, as you spend thinking about why they should love you. That's why it's important to be continually "tying a ribbon on it." That is, to be constantly and thought-fully wrapping up the experience of actually being one of your patients. Then sharing those beautifully wrapped packages.

The goal here is to use social media marketing to both consciously and subconsciously remind patients that they made a very good decision when they chose you as their healthcare provider. As you get better at articulating and distributing these gifts (your story), existing patients get better at internalizing and believing your story. They start thinking of themselves as members of your tribe.

Silence and/or apathy here results in missed opportunities to retain. Social media marketing provides these opportunities.

3. INCREASED PATIENT SPEND

GREATER TREATMENT ACCEPTANCE

The term "million-dollar filing cabinet" is used to describe most practices' frustration with the enormous body of recommended, yet unsched-uled treatment sitting inside hundreds of patient file folders. Social media marketing provides the opportunity to better educate patients on the value of accepting those treatment recommendations. In some cases, it's a long-term drip strategy. In other cases strategies may be more time sensitive.

REDUCING BROKEN APPOINTMENTS

As you well know, the negative financial impact of broken appointments can be enormous. Even a small handful of broken appointments can result in thousands of dollars in lost revenue each week.

Social media marketing can help you do two very important things in your efforts to overcome this challenge.

First, social media marketing helps place higher perceived value on routine care. For example, many of our client practices regularly publish content about oral cancer dangers. When patients are more knowledgeable about the risks of oral cancer, and when they understand how regular checkups can detect early warning signs, they're more likely to prioritize their checkups. Other practices shoot simple videos in which a hygienist talks about things like periodontal disease and the value of regular cleanings.

Second, when the relationship between the practice and patient is strengthened through social media strategies, patient loyalty to the practice increases.

Once in a while I find myself privy to conversations between dentists where some patient bashing goes on. I hear things like, "I'm going to start requiring a credit card number when patients book appointments, and then I'll charge their card if they don't show up!"

Hmmm... My thought? When patients (yes, friends) are loyal, they show up.

In my own personal case, I enjoy a great relationship with my dentist. I wouldn't dream of spacing off an appointment with them. I'm a loyal patient. How about instead of penalizing patients, strengthen your relationships with them so they become increasingly loyal and stop missing appointments. Social media marketing can help you do that.

KNOWING WHAT YOU DO

Let me illustrate this idea with a story. A man finds himself in need of a crown repair after an unfortunate incident with a popcorn kernel. He loves his dentist, but the first thing that comes to his mind is an advertisement he recently saw from another practice in town offering same-day crowns. He says to himself, "Wow, I'd only have to miss work once instead of twice? Great!" as he schedules an appointment with the other practice.

Little does he know that his regular dentist does same-day crowns as well. In fact, she has the exact same system in her practice! He just didn't know!

Do you provide cold sore therapy in your practice? How about clear braces? Sleep apnea treatment? Dentures? Implants? Botox? The list goes on. Many times patients are completely unaware of the scope of services you provide.

Remember, your patients don't think about you nearly as often as you think about them. How would they know about all the services you provide anyway? Your practice isn't like a restaurant where you hand someone a menu each time they visit. Many of them only know that you clean their teeth a couple times a year, and if they get a toothache they should call you.

Social media marketing provides many, many effective ways to educate patients about all of your services. Prior to having easy access to these powerful social media tools it was much more diffi-cult to educate patients about the things you do.

CREATING DESIRE

Humans have many common behavioral threads. Understanding these threads can be helpful in social media marketing because we're always trying to align our marketing activities with our business objectives. We're trying to figure out what motivates people to action.

There are fascinating bodies of thought about what prompts people to take action. One notion that often helps me bring decision-making clarity to digital marketing strategies is something I call the "SFC Principle." It's based on the idea that

Connect the dots between your social media activites and your business objectives.

people only take action when you provide one of the following:

1. Solve a Problem
2. Fill a Want or Need
3. Create Desire

Some patients only go to the dentist if they get a toothache. They have a problem and the dentist is there to solve their problem. These patients spend very little on dental care.

Some patients recognize the need for good oral health. They're the ones who visit you regularly for cleanings and checkups. They understand the value of preventative care. And, when dental problems come up, they have you fix them. For these patients, you're there to fill their need (or want) for sound oral health.

The patients who spend the most in our practices are often the ones who value many of the things you're capable of providing. They're often the ones in which you've created desire. For example, the desire for a drop-dead gorgeous smile makeover that prompts strangers to say, "Wow... You have an incredible smile!" The more successful we are as marketers in moving patients from #1 toward #2, and then from #2 toward #3, the more patients spend inside our practices. Social media marketing can help move them.

Now, to be clear, I'm not suggesting that one of your practice values should be doing everything you can to get patients to spend more money in your practice. That's not the point. The point I'm making goes back to this book's preface, where I said, "When your social media marketing activities are in harmony with your practice values and business objectives you have a credible claim to transformation and growth." You must decide what your priorities are, then align your social media activities with those priorities. I'm not here to tell you what your practice values or business objectives should be.

But, what I do know is this... When people place greater value on their dental care, it's reflected in how they spend their discretionary income.

Consider how much money people spend on hair care and tattoos each year. Billions! As a dental professional, you know that one of the best ways to put discretionary money to use to improve appearance and self-confidence is to invest in one's smile. Many studies support that premise.

However, patients don't always think the way we do, right? In part, flourishing practices achieve increased spend by adjusting patient mentality (focusing not on what you make, but what you make possible). Use social media marketing to tell the stories that create desire. Use social media marketing to position what you do, why it matters, and how it changes people's lives.

STARTING WITH "THE WHY"

When it comes to transitioning your practice's growth efforts from old school to new marketing, it's critical to grasp and embrace the concepts we've covered here in chapter one. It's the only way you'll be able to connect the dots, in your head, between your social media marketing activities and your business objectives. It's the only way you'll stay resolute and consistent. It's the only way you'll inspire your team and patients to participate.

In chapter two, we'll look at the six principles of effective dental social media marketing that bring clarity to what social media marketing is (and isn't) for dental practices. The goal is to use each of the principles we are about to talk about to help transform, and in turn grow, your flourishing practice.

02 CHAPTER TWO
The Six Principles of Effective
Dental Social Media Marketing

—

*O*nce we begin to get a foundational grasp on why social media marketing is important in both the transformation and growth of flourishing practices, we need to turn to "the what." A clear understanding of what social media marketing is (and equally important, what it isn't) provides the structural framework for the strategies and tactics to come.

I mentioned in the introduction that this book is about mindset, not tools. This chapter is about principles, not tactics.

Marketing isn't perfect. It's fickle. It's discouraging and difficult. If it were easy, every practice would be good at it, right? You'll get base hits and doubles quite often. You'll get an occasional home run too. And yes, you're gonna strike out sometimes.

Bank on that right now! The victories come through embracing the things you're learning. It makes us better marketers.

Over the last nine years, working with thousands of client practices, we've learned a thing or two about what works and what doesn't work when it comes to using dental social media marketing to transform and grow practices. That wealth of knowledge has come from real-life, practical, specific and concrete experiences with practices. Based on those experiences, I've distilled what I believe are the six fundamental principles that drive results.

Very soon you'll move from theory to application. Your foundational understanding of what dental social media marketing really is, exemplified through these six principles, will sustain you through your practical application efforts. On those days when you're down in the nitty-gritty social media weeds, struggling to remember why you're doing what you're doing, these ideas will sustain, encourage, and energize you. They'll keep you pointed in the right direction.

One more thought... As you come to embrace these six principles, remember: Your practice's interpretation of them will be unique, as will be your practical application of them. Your practice doesn't need to (nor should it) look like anyone else's practice in order to achieve social media marketing success.

You've likely seen examples where practices have been super successful doing one thing or another, and you may have thought, "Well, we could never do that because that's just not us." You're right, in part. Different strategies are better suited to different practices. But the underlying principles remain the same. Although a strong social media presence will include applying most, if not all of the six principles below, there may be some that your practice will naturally focus on more than others. And that's OK.

PRINCIPLE 1:
FIRST, GIVE AND PROVIDE VALUE

What does it mean to be a truly giving practice, and what does this have to do with social media marketing?

Giving is one of those things that makes life—and running a flourishing dental practice—fulfilling. And I don't just mean the kind of charitable giving associated with donating money or time. Constantly expressing gratitude, providing value to others, demonstrating empathy, and recognizing the efforts of team members are other important components of becoming a giving practice.

Social media has become the vehicle by which you can not only publish these share-worthy efforts, but you can also reinforce this mentality in the hearts and minds of everyone you're associated with—including patients, team members and the people in your community.

In an interview I recently conducted with our friend and client, Dr. Craig Spodak, he remarked, "I believe that the ultimate purpose of business is to provide compassion, trust, and love. We're not in business to just make money. Money is simply the consequence, or byproduct, of doing something with love. Everything we do [in our practice] is born from the desire to create a sense of community, whether that's within our office, with our patients, or in the actual neighborhoods that our practice serves."

Now I know what some of you are thinking... "Sure, that sounds nice, Jack. But unless it's going to improve my bottom line I can't make it a priority."

The good news is that it *will* improve your bottom line. Becoming a giving practice transforms your practice and team culture into something patients are proud of, and willing to share with others. And with smart integration of social media marketing into your giving efforts, you'll see the love you give come back through greater top-of-mind awareness, added goodwill, strengthened patient relationships and increased word-of-mouth referrals.

These six social media principles will keep you pointed in **the right** direction.

PASSION IS

CONTAGIOUS

EMPATHY

It can be tempting to take a cynical view of rising generations. "They're only interested in instant gratification, and they only care about themselves." Admit it; you've either thought it yourself, or you've heard others complaining about it. However, the actual trends tell a different story.

More and more often, brands are using empathy to appeal to new consumers because more and more often, customers care deeply about the empathetic, human element behind a brand. They want to know that the business they're supporting is a force for good in the world. A recent survey showed that 9 out of 10 millenials say that they would switch their business loyalty to support a business associated with a worthy cause.

When customers or patients empathize with a purpose or cause, they're significantly more likely to actively participate in building up the business—talking it up to their friends, giving recommendations, and sharing information.

Sometimes, it even translates into patients and customers taking up the cause themselves, enacting change in their own circles and communities. And when customers are engaged in a charitable cause that you promote or sponsor, they're also engaged in your brand.

CONNECTING WITH THE COMMUNITY

We can all feel isolated sometimes in our own little corners of the world. Technology may feel like it separates us more than it connects us. But that's less likely when your social media marketing efforts are integrated into communities. Online marketing and local community outreach might seem to be two completely different realms, but social media is a bridge that connects them.

Humans are social creatures who thrive in social groups. When you connect your social media marketing efforts with local outreach and a giving spirit, you tap something powerful that becomes cyclical. Social media helps you to get the word out and garner more support for your giving efforts. And

Social media connects your marketing effort

to your local community outreach efforts.

promoting these efforts online boosts attention, which leads to even more community connections.

Have you read Dale Carnegie's book, "How to Win Friends & Influence People"? If not, please do. It was written in the 1930s, but the book's principles clearly apply to social media marketing today! In his book, Dale says, "You can make more friends in two months by becoming interested in other people than you can in two years by trying to get other people interested in you." Many of our practice clients take this advice to heart by creating and sharing social media content that builds other people's businesses in their communities. Does that sound crazy? Remember, other businesses are connected to tribes of people as well! Take Dale's advice and show interest in others.

THE SPIRIT OF GIVING

Excuse me for being a bit mushy here. There's something important to be said about the positive spirit that giving brings into your practice. Expressing gratitude begets gratitude.

Social media posts can help us notice the amazing small details of life that remind us of how blessed we are. Emphasizing the positive de-emphasizes the negative. As your team's engagement in the spirit of giving increases, both patient and team member retention go up simply because people feel grateful that they're part of something bigger. And you'll feel it too.

Erich Fromm, an early 20th century sociologist said, "In the very act of giving... I experience myself as overflowing, spending, alive, hence as joyous. Giving is more joyous than receiving, not because it is a deprivation, but because in the act of giving lies the expression of my aliveness."

Becoming a giving practice is an integral part of becoming a flourishing practice. Social media marketing can help you with this. And although you may have already been doing these things for many, many years—long before there was social media— having these amazing new marketing tools can help you do much more, in much more efficient and effective ways.

Expressing gratitude **begets** gratitude.

PRINCIPLE 2: PARTICIPATION

I still see a lot of practices become convinced that social media marketing is important, but then make a common, critical mistake. They view new marketing the way they viewed old marketing—that is, "I write a check, then I forget about it. Yea!" After all, that's the way it always worked with the yellow pages and those direct mail postcards, right?

The sad part is that many of these practices sincerely believe that, finally, they "have" social media! However, social media isn't something you "have", it's something you "do." To be truly effective, social media marketing requires a certain level of participation.

YOUR "CHAMPION"

In most practices, the social media marketing efforts are spearheaded by a single individual. Often this is a practice manager, a team member who enjoys social media, or sometimes the doctor him/herself. Once in a while I see a spouse or other outside family member step in, coming into the practice a few times a week to work on social media.

Whoever it is, we always recommend that there's a specific point person who's responsible for the practice's social media accounts. When everybody's in charge, nobody's in charge. Who it is doesn't necessarily matter, as long as it is someone who has an open mind and giving heart, who personally participates inside the practice, and who is willing to be consistent and spend a little time learning.

Can you rotate champions? Of course! Just be sure it's clear who is responsible for what, and when.

> Social media isn't something you have.
> It's something you do.

YOUR TEAM

Having a champion is important, but if he or she is the only person in the practice who participates in social media, your practice isn't going to see optimal results. Social media marketing really is a team effort, and it will best contribute to your flourishing practice when more team members are involved.

Team participation means different things in different practices. In some cases it means that team members are willing to visit with patients from time to time about your practice's social media efforts. In other practices it means that team members are willing to contribute to writing a short blog post about something they enjoy doing outside of work. In some practices team participation means helping brainstorm ways the whole practice can bring social media into daily activities. In other practices it may mean having a hygienist shoot a short dental health tips video. And of course there are always engaging photo opportunities with other team members and/or with patients.

One more thought about team participation... Hopefully the doctor won't make him or herself exempt from participation! He or she is the face that every patient sees, and the connecting point between existing and prospective new patients. I don't mean that he or she must participate in everything. I mean that he or she should participate in some things. When the lead singer is involved, it's a lot easier to get the whole band to play. Time and time again, we've observed that those practices that do the best are the ones where the dentist is willing (at least to some extent) to participate.

YOUR PATIENTS

We're going to talk a lot more about this participation component in chapter 3. As a teaser, let's just say that if you're not seeing the social media marketing effectiveness you'd like to be seeing, in all likelihood your patients aren't participating with you while they're visiting your practice. Read on.

PRINCIPLE 3: INDUSTRY PARTNERING

No practice is an island. No practice flourishes alone. Your business is part of a larger industry ecosystem. Consider your professional relationships. Many of these companies, and the people you are connected to in these companies, are also striving to provide content that's valuable to their followers (and in turn, may be valuable to you). They're also nurturing relationships online and working to increase their reach and their clout.

You'll find that some of your best social media marketing traction can happen through these partnerships. For example, each year, hundreds of practices partner with the Smiles For Life Foundation to raise funds for children's charities through teeth whitening. By joining forces with others in dentistry, you're able to leverage each other's online reach and build relationships that serve your practice.

These dental industry partners may include...

PROFESSIONAL ORGANIZATIONS

Your membership in organizations such as the American Academy of Cosmetic Dentistry, Oral Cancer Cause, the Eco-Dentistry Association, the Crown Council, or the American Association of Orthodontics can create unexpected social media marketing opportunities.

NO PRACTICE FLOURISHES

ALONE.

SUPPLIERS

Who provides your equipment, materials, and clinical tools? Many times you'll find that these companies have a strong online presence and they may be eager to partner with you to sponsor a community event.

OTHER CLINICIANS

If you're a dentist, do you send some patients to endodontists, prosthodontists, or oral surgeons? Are you connected with them online? Are you showing interest in the things they're doing? Even helping to support and promote those things when appropriate?

And it goes both ways! If you're an endodontist, prosthodontist or oral surgeon, are you digitally engaged with the dentists in your community? Are you connected with each of them on LinkedIn, for example? When you connect with people online, you'll find that the relationships can be mutually beneficial.

COMMUNITY RELATIONSHIPS

Every dental practice is a location-based business, which means that your ties with the local community are a valuable asset. Hook up on social media with local government agencies, non-profits, and other local businesses to join the conversation about local events and concerns.

PRINCIPLE 4: TRUST BUILDING

In social media marketing, there's a difference between just getting attention and building trust. Sure, garnering attention is an important component of marketing. But compromising trust to get attention can jeopardize a practice's brand.

For example, occasionally I'll see a practice chasing that ever-elusive "viral" campaign or video. And while some good can come from getting that kind of buzz, having that as the goal is rarely a good bet. If what you're considering won't actually move someone closer to wanting to become your patient or to feel more loyalty to your practice, then all that attention is of very little value.

So instead of just waving your hands in the air to get as many eyes on you as possible, look into techniques that actually build trust. Find your practice's "sweet spot" in doing that too.

KEEP IT FUN

Now and then, social media posts are simply meant to bring a smile to someone's face. And that's enough! When you're having fun in the practice and on social media, your patients will respond. The effectiveness in achieving marketing objectives between practices that participate in a few fun activities on social media, and those who are afraid to do so, is like night and day.

REMEMBER WHY PEOPLE ARE THERE

I promise you that zero percent of your patient base, and zero percent of the people who live in your community, opened a personal Instagram account so they could learn what dental advice you have for them. Remember why most people use social media! Nobody initially signs up with the purpose in mind of helping their favorite brands promote themselves.

For the most part, people engage on social media to connect, find value, and have fun.

FUN IS CONTAGIOUS

I know this may sound strange. Once practices really start understanding how social media works, and they start "getting into it," most of them actually start loving marketing. In part, that's simply because it's fun. Yes, it's fun to think about how to engage your patients, how to attract their interests, and how to tell your practice's story. Instead of obsessing over old-school, formulaic marketing techniques—many of which really have no application to new marketing—ask yourself this simple question: are you having fun? If you are, the odds are pretty good that your patients are having fun too... And fun spreads. Life is short. Relieve some pressure. Do what works.

Fun doesn't have to be silly. Fun doesn't mean unprofessional. Fun doesn't mean stupid.

There are so many tools and techniques that you can use to bring fun into your practice and your social media marketing. We provide tons of specific tools and ideas on our website.

BE HUMAN & PERSONAL

You know those moments when small talk evolves into a real discussion? Those moments when you share something honest about yourself and what's going on with your life, and suddenly there's a deeper connection between you and the person you're visiting with? Most of us spend our time on social media engaged in small talk. And while small talk is an important part of relationship-building, it doesn't have the emotional power that comes when we get personal.

I've seen some of the best patient engagement on social media take place when a dentist shared a thumbs-up from a hospital bed after emergency surgery, and when a sweet hygienist announced the gender of her baby just before taking her maternity leave. Could you talk about a fun hobby you have, or feature your beloved canine companion on National Dog Day?

Create posts congratulating team members on personal accomplishments, asking them a few questions about their interests, or simply showing how much they enjoy working in your practice.

Social media helps patients know **you care** even when they're not in **your chair.**

Share things that demonstrate how much you care about your relationships with patients! Choose a "Patient of the Day" or "Patient of the Week," snap and share a photo with them and caption it with one or two lines about why you're glad to see them when they visit. Small appreciation gestures go a long way in not only building rapport with individuals, but also showing prospective new patients how much you treasure patient relationships, and that you're truly committed to your patients' well-being.

Now, nobody should feel pressured to share things. But you'll often find that when you and your team members open up, patients are actually interested and

Professional can also
be **approachable.**

happy to learn more about you. Build a more compelling social media presence by focusing on the needs, interests, and personalities of your patients and team members. Not only is this more engaging content for patients and fans, it's much more fun for your team to create as well!

BE SINCERE & TRANSPARENT

Consider what it is that makes you trust a person, or a business. Consider this anecdote from one of our long-time clients and friends, Dr. Adrian Fenderson: "A new patient recently chose me because he said I appeared to be so 'available and open'—not hiding from my patients. That same person said that a dentist who is transparent and accessible is the kind he wanted."

Many dentists, as health professionals, feel that they need to put on a sort of "front" in order to inspire confidence. For some, social media may seem to threaten that—especially when I'm asking you to be personal, sincere, and transparent. However, these are exactly the things that most patients desire, far more than a stiff upper lip and an impenetrable professional facade. You ask your patients to be honest with you when they report medical history, habits, and concerns, right? Do you honor them with the same honesty and approachability?

CLOUT'S POWER

Now, while you're being transparent, human, personal, honest, sincere, and fun (whew!) you're also people's trusted healthcare partner and professional. Your training and experience uniquely qualify you to advise and care for your valued patients. That's why it's okay, on occasion, to toot your horn and talk about the important clinical things you do.

There are many things that increase your professional clout and make you the trusted doctor that you are. This not only includes your qualifications, but also the books you read, the CE you attend and complete, the professional journals you subscribe to, the organizations you belong to, the lectures you give, the conferences or forums you participate in, and the blogs you read. All of these things can be sources for raw materials and experiences that you can use to create social media marketing content for your audiences.

Also, don't think that you have to create everything from scratch. Many doctors that I work with make a habit of sharing the things that they're reading and learning about with their audiences through social media. For example, did you just read an informative article over the weekend, in a professional journal that you subscribe to, that brings greater clarity to the topic of oral cancer? If so, share your thoughts about it! It means a lot to the people who trust you. You don't have to write the article from scratch yourself. Just link to the article and write a short paragraph about how important it is to you, personally, that your valued patients and friends understand this important topic. Ask them to read it as well, and if they have questions, ask them to call you to discuss them.

PRINCIPLE 5:
YOUR DIGITAL FOOTPRINT

Dental digital marketing is like owning online real estate—your own little corner of the internet. You can't really "control" it. At least not completely. But you can help steer it.

Conversations about your practice are likely already happening online whether you are participating in them or not. People are actively contributing to the positive or negative buzz that surrounds local businesses through reviews, tags, and social media posts. Healthcare professionals should be especially sensitive to this reality. Whether or not you're present to contribute to those conversations, your current patients, former patients and prospective new patients may all be creating your practice's digital footprint for you.

Today, search engines are very interested in social media content. They didn't used to be. It's not uncommon now for a practice's business accounts to show up early in search results. Sometimes the dentist's personal accounts, such as a LinkedIn profile, will show up too.

It's time to join the conversation and own the story that's told about your practice online. Your website will help patients look up your address and hours but it will never build connections, enable referrals, strengthen relationships or encourage patient advocacy the way social media can.

PRINCIPLE 6: CONSISTENCY

There are lots of different kinds of social media content. Some types have a longer "shelf life" than do other types. For example, some videos you produce may only be relevant and useful while something is trending. Others, such as an office tour video are considered "evergreen." Sometimes, social media marketing is like publishing a newspaper, and sometimes it's like publishing a book. Some blog posts are out of date within a month or two and others can engage audiences for years.

That's why consistency is so important to your social media marketing success. When you're reliable and consistent online, it increases your patients' trust in what you're doing.

Transference takes place in patients' minds when they see a practice that's consistent. The assumption is that if you're consistent and reliable in providing relevant, educational, honest human content through your social media platform that you also likely provide the same consistency and leading-edge standards in everything you do—including the dental materials and procedures you use, the patient benefit-driven technologies you ascribe to, the way you respond to and treat people, the CE you attend, etc.

Staying consistent in your social media marketing activity can be tough. I understand. But it's easier when you're doing the things we're talking about in this book. And, it can be easier when you have a little outside help. If you're one of our valued clients, we make it much easier for you to be consistent. However, if you're not our client, you can still achieve consistency by making it a priority and considering the following three things:

BE PATIENT

Your patient won't eradicate gingivitis with one night's flossing, and you won't get hundreds of followers with one post. Give it time.

CELEBRATE SMALL VICTORIES

That click from one follower isn't just a number in the corner of your post. It's a human you've touched. Even one engaged patient can become invaluable to your practice. Why? Because you haven't just engaged her. You've potentially earned permission to engage with her trusted, highly scalable, permission-based social networks.

DO SOMETHING DAILY

Dedicate a small amount time each day. And, once a week, find 30 minutes to do something a little extra.

"THE WHAT": YOUR SAFE ZONE

In chapter one we looked at "the why". Here in chapter two we looked at the six principles that bring clarity to what social media marketing is for dental practices ("the what").

Consider these six principles together, as your social media marketing safe zone. When your marketing isn't working as well as you'd like, return to your safe zone and re-evaluate your efforts. Look carefully at each principle and brainstorm with your team. Perhaps you'll want to de-emphasize one of the principles a little bit and focus a little bit more effort on another one for a period of time.

When these six principles become your compass, the day-to-day tactics themselves make more sense, and they become easier to execute. You start doing the right things for the right reasons, and it becomes much more likely that you'll stay consistent, which leads to greater success.

In chapter three, we'll talk about a 3-part strategy for effective execution, "the how."

When your marketing isn't working
as well as you'd like, return to your
safe zone and **re-evaluate your efforts.**

03

CHAPTER THREE
A Simple 3-Part Strategy

—

*I*t's time to get to work. You know why social media marketing is important and you're clear about what social media marketing really is and what it isn't. But now you're asking yourself, "Is there some sort of formula or strategy for actually doing it effectively?" Yes, there is.

I'm confident that you're starting to feel gung-ho about social media marketing. But, you're also feeling afraid that achieving any measure of success will take far more time than you have available. I understand those conflicting feelings. I hear this concern a lot. Let me assure you right now that you can do this without it having to take too much of your valuable time. Trust me.

ABOUT TIME

It's about time, right? Having worked with a myriad of practices, when it comes to addressing the fear about how much time this will take, here's what I've learned. Most of this fear results from the experiences people have had in not knowing what to do. Did that last sentence sink in? This is important, so let me say it again, in a little different way. It's not that effective social media marketing takes a lot of time. It's that most practices don't know what to do, or how to be effective, in the small amounts of time they have to do it. In other words, if the champion in your practice can only carve out 10 minutes a day for social media marketing, she can be super effective in 10 minutes if she has a plan and knows exactly what to do. Unfortunately, what often happens is that she spends those 10 minutes frantically bouncing around the web looking for another cat video to post and when she can't find anything good, she gets discouraged and gives up. The result of these bad experiences leads her to the conclusion that, "social media just takes too much time."

Each month at My Social Practice we feature a "Practice of the Month" on our blog and honor that practice for the great job they're doing with their social media marketing. As part of interviewing them for the blog post, we ask them how much time they typically spend on their social media marketing each week. Now remember, these are practices that are absolutely nailing it! The cream of the crop! The examples we hold up for inspiration! On average, these remarkable practices are spending 2–3 hours a week. No kidding. They're spending 15–20 minutes a day, and then they're carving out an extra hour sometime during the week to do "something more." The secret is that they know exactly what to do during the little amounts of time they spend.

You can do this too. Stick to my simple 3-part strategy: **1) Create a post, 2) invite a patient, then 3) distribute the content.** I promise you'll see real results if you just do these three things with a little fortitude, consistency and passion.

We've laid a lot of theoretical groundwork in chapters one and two that supports this strategy. Here's where the rubber meets the road.

CREATE.
INVITE.
DISTRIBUTE.
CREATE.
INVITE.
DISTRIBUTE.

CREATE A POST

Your first task is to create a post. Now before you start getting all nervous and worried about this word "create," let me explain.

Creating a post doesn't necessarily mean you're always creating that post from scratch. You might be creating the post from scratch that day, but you might not be. It's OK sometimes to share something that you didn't create yourself from scratch. Of course, the more original posts that you can create yourself, the better. And you will keep getting better and better at doing that. But certainly in the beginning, let's be real, practical, and honest about this. When you're first starting out, for most practices, it's tough to do something amazing and original every single time. That's OK! Baby steps! This isn't a race, it's a journey. A process.

Did I just take a little bit of pressure off of you? Did it feel good? I hope so, but don't get too comfortable.

Although you may not be creating every single post from scratch in the beginning, I'm encouraging you to always be working toward that goal. Taking a photo of a team member, with or without a patient, is an example of a post created from scratch. Sharing a link to an interesting, valuable article you read is an example of a post that you don't create from scratch. If you share a link, it's important to write a quick personal comment to accompany it, such as, "I just read this great blog post about the dangers of oral cancer. I'd like you to read it too, and if you have questions, let me know." In other words, you've personalized your post, but you didn't create it from scratch.

MAKE POSTS WORTH THEIR TIME

Today, posting social media content is sometimes referred to as "content marketing." Content marketing simply means that you're creating and sharing content that engages, informs, and sparks interest, without necessarily pushing a specific agenda and without directly selling stuff. Generally

Did I just take a bit of **pressure off** of you?
Did it feel good? I hope so, but dont get **too comfortable.**

speaking, the majority of the content you create and post should provide value to people; it shouldn't be a sales pitch.

One of the best ways to know whether or not your content is providing value is to ask yourself this simple question: "Is this something that I would value in my own social media feed?"

Ask yourself, "Is what I'm about to post something I would **find value** in myself?"

Search engines and social media platforms just keep getting smarter. Trying to manipulate them into giving visibility to subpar content is increasingly ineffective. Instead, social media platforms give priority to content that meets people's needs and desires, connects them with other people (and sometimes, brands), and is relevant to their interests and/or communities. And when people come across that type of content, they're more likely to engage with it—which means more sharing, more value for both sides, and greater reach.

SHAREWORTHINESS

Some brands hijack social media to garner attention with clickbait. Other brands use social media to feed the internet's insatiable appetite for another cat video. And many brands use social media to beat their chests and self-promote 24/7. However, none of these strategies lead to sustained relationships built on trust. Flourishing practices use social media to actually provide value to their friends and followers. And to do that, your content needs to be shareworthy.

What makes something shareworthy? It's pretty simple, really. People actually care about it! When you give people a reason to care, you give them a reason to share. So, what (and who) do people care about?

FIRST, THEMSELVES—IT'S HUMAN NATURE

Would you walk into a cocktail party, climb up on the bar with a megaphone and start telling people to stop doing whatever it is they're doing, so they can come over and talk to you because you're the most interesting person in the room? Of course not— unless you're just a clueless jerk.

You've heard the old saying "People don't care how much you know until they know how much you care." This is especially true on social media. Instead of spending your time on off-putting self-promotion, consider the other side of this virtual relationship. Try being interested, instead of interesting. Create things that help you connect with people, then start conversations using social media. Learn more about your patients—and prospective new patients—as real people first. Continually ask yourself what your followers are getting from their social media relationship with you. What's in it for them?

In addition, when your patients are browsing through social media feeds, consider their mindset in those moments. They are there to learn about their friends, to share information about themselves, to discover things that are valuable to them, to participate in local events and issues, and to keep up with valued relationships. That's why you'll see better results when the things you publish directly or indirectly support the things that they're doing. Is it OK once in while to simply share something on social media that does nothing more than bring a smile to

INTERESTED > INTERESTING

someone's face? Of course! Doing so may not provide huge value, but it can be stress relieving, memorable and shareworthy. Just remember, you're not the host. You're a guest at their dinner table.

SECOND, YOU

I hope you're starting to see that you can't expect people to share something simply because you put it out there. That's not enough. There are far too many things vying for people's attention. They have to care about it. And believe it or not, YES!... Many of them actually care about you too when you show interest in them first. They may not always care about dry dental facts, but they usually care about the people in your practice with whom they have personal relationships. That's why a staple in every effective social media content plan includes posts and photos about your team sharing their professional and/or personal moments.

DIFFERENT POSTS HAVE DIFFERENT PURPOSES

When you're considering the type of content to share on social media, should you prioritize fun or facts? Is asking questions or posting photos more important? Perhaps you've already seen some success with certain kinds of posts you've done in the past. That's great! But before you start leaning too heavily on just one type of post, keep in mind that you really need variety to achieve a well-rounded social media presence.

Dental social media strategies and tactics have a number of different objectives, and not every single post will serve each of those objectives in the same way. One day's post may be meant to simply trigger a smile and garner an engagement. Another day's post may be meant to highlight something about your practice culture. Some days will be about featuring a service that you offer, and other days will be about oral health education. Some days will simply be about fun.

In my years working with thousands of practices, I've identified six general characteristics of effective content. It isn't that every single thing you publish needs to have each of these characteristics! That's not my point. It's that effective posts usually include one (or more) of these six characteristics:

Just remember, you're not the host. **You're a guest** at their dinner table.

THEY ENGAGE

Most of the time, these posts don't even have anything to do with dentistry. They simply invite patients to participate and keep them involved with your practice. Engagement creates a snowball effect on social media, meaning that if someone engages with your post today, there's greater likelihood they'll see and engage with your content in the future. Many times these are posts that reference something that's trending elsewhere on social media.

THEY PROVIDE VALUE

As a dental professional, you have knowledge that can benefit your patients' health and personal care. This can include information such as what the attributes of a good toothpaste are, or when a parent should be concerned about a child's thumbsucking habit. Also, there are many non-dental topics you can talk about that provide value. Is the county fair next month an important event in your community? Perhaps you know the best place in town to get discounted admission tickets! Share that information. It provides value.

THEY SHOW PRACTICE CULTURE

Your practice is unique because your team members are unique. Patients love seeing familiar faces and becoming "insiders" on those moments that make up your practice's story. When the things you publish promote your practice's culture, it helps people connect with you on a personal level. Are you involved in charitable activities? Use social media to not only help people learn more about practice culture, but to increase the effectiveness of your charitable efforts as well.

THEY BOOST CLOUT

The internet is noisy, with lots of unreliable information. When you speak out as your patients' trusted professional on the topics you know best, it increases your clout, and reminds people that they have a resource they can trust. And this isn't just about the doctor... Other team members can add value here as well. Identify things that each team member can contribute that will boost the credibility of the practice. Occasionally, you may want to shoot a short, informal video about a specific technology you use in the practice—such as your new laser. Don't get too technical or long-winded about it. Just be person-able. In addition, take opportunities to talk about the CE you attend and why the knowledge you're gaining benefits your patients, not you.

Use social media to talk about dentistry **from your patient's point of view**, not from your point of view.

THEY DEMONSTRATE PASSION OR EMPATHY

Do you love what you do? Let your patients know! Take note of those moments that motivate and inspire you, and then share them with your followers. When we reveal the things we're most passionate about, we reveal our genuine selves. Is someone on your team running her first half marathon? Have her talk about it! These can be personal or professional passions and interests. And sometimes, just put yourself in your patients' shoes and express empathy. Try talking about dentistry and/or the experience of being your patient, from your patient's point of view, not yours. It can go a long way in building trust.

THEY STRENGTHEN RELATIONSHIPS

Invite meaningful conversations on social media, and utilize posts to strengthen existing relationships with your patients. Sometimes, when a dental professional is struggling to understand the value of social media marketing, they'll say, "I just don't get the ROI of social media marketing!" to which I reply, "What's the ROI of better relationships with your patients?" Every business owner clearly and intuitively understands the value there. Hands down, social media marketing is the very best way to scale your ability to strengthen relationships.

INVITE A PATIENT

Your second task is to invite a patient.

This one can feel more unfamiliar. The idea here is that you're not just handling the job of social media marketing yourself. Instead, you're empowering patients through the principle of advocacy and encouraging them to also create and publish content about your practice. These contributions are made through reviews, patient photos taken in your practice, and any post where your patient gives you a shout or talks about your practice inside their own trusted, permission-based, highly scalable social networks.

SOCIAL PROOF

Do you remember (or, have you heard of) the pioneer of hidden camera entertainment? It was a television show called "Candid Camera." Aside from being fun to watch, it revealed fascinating things about the way people think, what catches our attention, and why we act the way we act.

One of their most famous segments involved a group of actors on an elevator who all stood facing the back of the elevator, instead of facing forward.

The elevator, with the actors inside, traveled between floors picking up unsuspecting passengers. Consistently, after a little bit of initial confusion, passengers turned to face the rear of the elevator as well so as not to stand out from the rest of the people in the elevator. Some passengers even turned side to side, or took off their hats, when everyone else in the elevator did so.

It's amusing to see someone behave in a certain way for no other reason than "everyone else is doing it, so it must be the right thing to do." But it's kinda how we're wired. We're influenced by the people who surround us and they have a significant impact on behavior. We observe the actions of our friends, family, neighbors and colleagues when we make decisions or are in unfamiliar situations.

In new marketing terms, we call what happened in that elevator an example of "social proof." People often consider the actions and opinions of others as sufficient proof that such behavior is favorable or correct. Let's say a restaurant consistently has a line out the door. In the minds of many, that's enough to convince them that the food is good. Or if a star basketball player tweets about how much she loves her new shoes, her fans won't need to hear anything else to have a positive opinion of that brand's shoes.

> Your patients are your greatest marketing asset.

In the case of your practice, building social proof is an important part of attracting new patients, and retaining existing ones. In decisions as important as choosing an oral healthcare provider, people do their research and ask their friends—especially now that social media has made doing that so easy. What others are saying about you online—that social proof—may be the determining factor in whether or not people choose you as their dentist.

ADVOCACY

Effective dental social media marketing isn't about turning strangers into patients—it's about turning patients into advocates. Social media marketing is a conversation. It's not just about what you say; it's also about what your patients and followers have to contribute. Often, the most effective promotions won't come from you. On social media, each of your followers is empowered to become an ambassador. Many patients who love your practice are willing to say so. They'll leave you a review, take photos with your team, share your content, and speak up when a friend of theirs asks online for a dentist recommendation in her area.

A recent Nielsen "Global Trust in Advertising" report concluded that most people (83 percent) trust personal recommendations from friends more than any other form of promotion. Your patients are your greatest marketing asset. With audiences becoming more and more cynical about advertising and traditional marketing, you can't afford to neglect the power of patient advocacy through social media.

INFLUENCERS

Influencer marketing can be a cost-efficient way of getting expert and micro-celebrity social proof. Today, this is most prevalent on platforms

It's not about turning strangers into patients.

It's about turning **patients into advocates.**

like Instagram. Brands often sponsor micro-influ-encers—people with a strong social media influence who aren't well-known celebrities—and have them post about their products.

It's actually quite simple to find and reach out to local influencers of all types through social media. If you offer them a special discount on whitening or other dental treatment in exchange for them posting about you on social media, make sure that both you and the influencer are transparent about the nature of the promotion. It's important that influencers disclose that he or she has received compensation. It's often as simple as placing #ad or #sponsored in the caption.

MAKE IT EASY

Although most patients are happy to participate in your social media marketing, they're not likely to go very far out of their way to do so. All of the usual hurdles that prevent you from posting on a busy morning will affect them too, and they won't just automatically be as motivated as you are. So, clear those hurdles for them.

At My Social Practice, we equip our clients with tools that smooth out the way for "inviting" including in-office photo booths and a reviews platform that invites patients to write reviews while they're visiting your practice. But even if you aren't our client, you can easily empower patient advocacy. Have a tablet available in the waiting area where patients can leave you a review before they go home and forget. Prompt fun photo taking with props and signs, and single out a corner of your practice with good lighting and a great background so that you get beautiful snapshots your patients are willing to share.

THE IMPORTANCE OF REVIEWS

92 percent of customers read online reviews and 88 percent report that these reviews make a major impact on their purchasing decisions. 85 percent of them say that they trust online reviews as much as a personal recommendation. And guess what? Social media sites are among the most-trusted resources for reviews. Every review that a patient leaves for your practice is golden, and practices that under-

stand the need for invitation marketing are actively engaged in establishing robust review pages as part of their digital footprint.

What about negative reviews and comments? Many practices can't help but feel a little trepidation about reviews. After all, what if they're not all positive? Well, if you're trying to avoid and filter negative comments at all costs, you're actually missing out on an opportunity. The presence of negative reviews can actually boost trust in the validity of your reviews, as long as negative comments are very much overpowered by the positive ones. Just be smart in how you handle them. Remember, you're not necessarily responding to a negative review for the benefit of the person who wrote it, although that's certainly part of it. But because hundreds, if not thousands of other people may see how you responded and then form opinions about you based on your response, it's important to handle such reviews with care. A good way to learn how to do that is to simply watch how others do it, especially in hospitality industries. Also, at My Social Practice, we offer free ebooks and blog posts that can help you.

One of the best things about reviews on social media is that you're able to actively participate in feedback from patients. Your responses add context to specific reviews, and readers are able to view your patient service approach first hand. Even if a review includes a complaint about your practice, a professional and compassionate response can elevate a reader's opinion of your practice. Embrace these opportunities.

CHERRY PICK

Contrary to how some dental practices may feel initially, it's not pushy to simply invite selected patients to leave a review or to shoot and post a photo and tag your practice. I'm going to make it really easy with this 2-step guide to inviting:

YOUR APPOINTMENT SCHEDULE

Start with your appointment schedule. Each day, browse through your appointment schedule and identify one patient (or perhaps two or three, so you have a couple of backups) who you would be comfortable asking to help you out. Choose the patients you already have great relationships with!

Maybe they've been with your practice for years. Maybe they have an especially strong rapport with one of your team members. Or maybe you don't really know them yet, but you've done some special treatment for them that they have been very pleased with. In my opinion, your daily treatment schedule—that thing you look at all day, every day—is among your greatest marketing assets.

ASK IN THE RIGHT WAY

When these star patients come in for their appointments, invite them to act as advocates for your practice by saying something like, "Susan, you've been our patient for many years, and we love serving you and your family. We've noticed that we get more awesome patients just like you when someone like you publishes a photo from inside our practice, or writes a review about us. Would you consider doing that for us today?"

Identify, then ask. This 2-step plan get easier and easier to do every time you do it. Why? Because the majority of your patients are happy to support your practice—especially when you cherry pick the ones that love you. You'll be amazed at the positive feedback you get when you simply ask. These conversations are actually easy when you already have a positive relationship. It just comes down to a one-on-one conversation that comfortably happens in your practice. And this doesn't take much time at all.

DISTRIBUTE THE CONTENT

Distribution works in tandem with creating a post, and inviting a patient (as explained above). Distribution is becoming more and more important for dental practices to understand because many social media platforms today are becoming "pay-to-play" business models.

PAID MEDIA'S EVOLUTION

Paid media is not dead. However, it's always changing. Many people have been predicting the end of paid media (a.k.a. advertising). This prediction is premature, as few other strategies have the immediacy and scale that paid media can have.

Your journey will include delightful and unexpected surprises, as well as painful disappointments.

There are still some principles of traditional advertising that hold true in this new marketing climate, such as the "Rule of 12," which suggests that future patients will need to be "touched" by your practice, by your message, by your culture, or by one of your existing patients up to a dozen times before they even notice you, remember anything about you, or take any kind of action. Does that feel discouraging? Sure. But here's the good news! Prior to having these amazing, easy-to-use and effective social media tools it was much, much more difficult to achieve these "touches."

So how does this tie into paid media? Often, the organic reach of your social media content is limited and sporadic unless you kickstart it through paid social. People have to actually see your content first, before you can expect them to engage with it. People can't share what they don't see. The viral potential of truly shareworthy content inside people's personal platforms is only unleashed by brands when the first people can initially see it, which means we still turn to paid promotion in jumpstart the impact we're looking for.

Most popular social media platforms were created without a specific revenue-generating agenda. However, as these companies have grown, they've learned to scale and monetize their networks. A social media platform's priority is to provide value to its users, which is why they will always prioritize content with a proven track record of popularity and value. However, as brands have entered this space, the social media platforms have learned to leverage access to users (a.k.a. your patients and followers). Brands unwilling to join the pay-to-play game are finding themselves pushed lower and lower in feed priority, to the point where their content may become invisible.

We won't treat this topic in detail here because it's constantly changing. Check out the most current, free downloadable ebooks and blog posts we publish at My Social Practice to learn more about this important topic. Understanding it is very important to your social media marketing success.

A PROMOTION CYCLE

Paid media's primary function in social media marketing is to act as a catalyst which, at key times, drives more engagement. Numerous books have been written about the "paid-owned-earned media" model. We won't dive deep here. But for our purposes it's helpful to have a high-level understanding of how different types of media feed each other to create a promotion cycle.

Most people are tempted to sort each kind of media into a separate bucket while they consider their promotional strategy. But smart marketers know that the paid-owned-earned model is cyclical. Paid distribution can give your owned media the boost it needs at certain moments to generate more earned buzz. If you can give your owned media enough presence (by first, making sure that the content is valuable and shareworthy enough to garner attention, and second, by actively distributing it through paid marketing) it can earn mentions, advocates, and fans who will continue to promote it, even after you've finished creating, publishing and promoting it yourself.

Forms of paid promotion are different from one social media tool to another, and because they change all the time, we won't go into any logistics here. However, understanding the importance of paid promotion is vital to your social media strategy, and will help you make the most of your generated content.

Use social media to achieve the level of reach that keeps you top-of-mind.

PAID MEDIA

Paid media is any media wherein the brand pays the platform owner to share the content or message. This includes things like banner ads, paid search, paid promotions, and paid social media advertising. It can also include paying to promote (boost) your social media content (which is owned media that you kickstart).

OWNED MEDIA

Owned media is created and published by you on your own accounts, i.e. all the things we talked about above under the section heading "Create A Post," including things like blog posts housed on your website, photos on your Instagram account, etc, etc.

EARNED MEDIA

Earned media is the buzz that's generated around your brand by others, without you having to pay for it. Earned media includes news coverage of events, unpaid mentions from bloggers and other influencers, and all that content we talked about above under the section heading "Invite A Patient," including all the comments, shares and re-shares that may result.

As social media tools evolve, the particulars of our strategies will as well. You won't stay on the leading edge by reading printed books, including this one (that's why it's important that you subscribe to the ongoing, free content we offer on our My Social Practice website). My confident prediction is that regardless of how tools evolve, this simple 3-part strategy for creating, inviting, and distributing great content will serve your social media marketing efforts well for a long time to come.

CONCLUSION

—

In chapter three I talked a little bit about our "Practices of the Month". For many years we've singled out one of our client practices each month to feature on our blog. This has included interviewing and learning from in-practice champions. Below, I'm including quotes from these champions. The intention isn't to promote our company's products or services. In other words, these are not testimonials specifically about My Social Practice. I've left those out because chest beating isn't this book's purpose.

These are testimonials to the power of social media marketing. And although I've excluded the champions' names and their practice names, these aren't fanciful things that I've written to impress you. They're actual, personal quotes—and I'm happy to share the specifics about who said them upon request. You can also read them on My Social Practice's blog.

As you read them, I want you to hear (and feel) their passion and advice. Read between the lines. Liken some of their applicable challenges and experiences to yours. Take courage in knowing that social media marketing success in dental and dental specialty practices isn't just a pipe dream. And although your practice's specific experiences and practical application will be very different than theirs, effectiveness is absolutely attainable.

WHAT THEY HAD TO SAY

"We love social media as a creative outlet to make dentistry not so scary, and present the doctor much more personable."

"Now we feel more confident in selling ourselves. Social media has helped us create a 'personality transition' to being more comfortable sharing—and sharing often!"

"Our patients who follow our social media accounts are our strongest patient referral sources. We also use social media to support them, and their businesses. It's great for networking."

"Sometimes it's hard to quantify the effects. We've gotten new patients, but it's more than that. It fits with our practice culture. It's another way for us to show our patients what we're all about."

"Our patients are more bonded to our practice. With a fragile economy, and insurance plans constantly changing, we truly value those relationships."

"Social media has us talking and interacting with patients outside of their six-month check ups which is hugely beneficial. It has definitely built a stronger sense of loyalty with our patients."

"Social media gives us a chance to display who we are. It's a foundation for future conversations and interactions."

"We get new patients from social media, but that's not the best part. We know almost everyone checks us out on Facebook to see what we're 'really like' before their first visit. We've truly build an online community of patients, parents, families and friends."

"We already had a well-established rapport/relationship with our patients, but social media has enabled us to take it much deeper."

"Don't be afraid to ask people to participate! It's alright if, occasionally, someone says 'no'. You'll be surprised to find that most people enjoy being involved."

"It's okay to tell people you're trying to build your social media pages! Most of our patients are thrilled to help!"

"People see what their friends and family are doing, and they're sold on your practice before they even come in because they trust the referring source."

"People can tell when it's real."

"Don't be afraid to get your team on board. Ask them to help support your efforts. They want you to succeed, and they'll do what they can to help!"

"Assume that your patients love you as much as you love them."

"Patients love our mix of educational and fun content."

"People love seeing us 'behind the scenes'."

"Many patients say that they feel the 'family atmosphere' in our practice, and that our social media pages reflect that too."

"We pull patients in and help them feel more like friends, rather than patients. Creating these relationships seems to make their office visits more relaxed and enjoyable."

"When our team traveled for training, we posted about it. We got so many comments from patients and non-patients saying things like, 'You guys look like you enjoy working together. I want to work there!' That made us feel good."

"We have better patient retention because of our social media. We feel more connected to our patients. We know their likes and dislikes. We know about their families and activities. When they come in, we feel closer connections with them!"

"The #1 benefit of our social media marketing efforts is reminding patients that we're always there for them whenever they need us."

"The best part is that we stay top-of-mind with patients. They think about us more often than twice a year. This makes them much more likely to remain patients. Social media is also great for exposure. The more times prospective new patients hear about us, the more likely they are to become patients—especially when their friends are posting about their great experiences at our office."

"The number one benefit is that we stay so in touch with our patients. They are constantly aware of what's going on in our practice and what we're doing to better our community."

"Social media keeps us relevant in the 21st century. We don't take being in business for granted. We're sharing with our community that we're evolving and modern. We've really made an impact through online, social media conversations."

"One new patient said that she saw how involved we were in our community, and from that she knew we would take good care of her and her family. We find that people care less about the work we do and more about the kind of people we are. Social media helps us communicate that."

"The greatest benefit of social media has been the influx of new patients seeking information about our practice. Friends and family members of our patients see that we're a family-friendly, high-tech practice without even stepping through the door. When potential new patients are looking for a dentist, they compile as much information as they can to make an informed decision."

"We use social media as a conversation starter."

"When a potential new patient sees us having fun doing our jobs and how happy our patients are, they're more likely to become our new patient."

"Our team members take an active role in show-casing the practice.They're proud of our social media posts! I never thought this would be a side benefit of social media marketing. I overhear patient comments that they've 'never seen people enjoy their job so much!' and 'I love coming in to see you guys!' You can't put a big enough dollar value on that. It directly affects patient retention and patient referrals."

"New patient acquisition is the #1 benefit for us. It's always awesome hearing that they've looked at our posts prior to coming in and that they've seen how much fun we have with our team and patients."

"We get compliments all the time on our social media. People mention that they've never seen a dental practice with such a great social media presence. We hear comments around our community from people saying they see our name on social media. That makes a huge difference! People have to see that you're legit and genuine. They need to hear your name lots of times before it sinks in!"

"I've been surprised how our social media has generated positive buzz and conversation throughout the community. The more our name is out there being tossed around, the more familiar and comfortable people are with coming to our office."

"As a result of our social media postings, our office has become quite renowned in our small town, and beyond! In fact, we're often stopped in public by patients and non-patients alike to comment on our videos and other social media posts."

"Our patients really love our posts that show pictures of us having fun in the office and in the community. These always generate the biggest response. People love seeing that we're down to earth and like to have fun just like them. It creates stronger relationships and loyalty with them. They like anything with a personal touch."

"A new patient recently chose me because he said I appeared to be so 'available and open'—not hiding from my patients. That same person said that a dentist who is transparent and accessible is the kind he wanted."

"We've been truly surprised by how many people our social media posts reach."

"Social media is providing a great way for us to create a 'history' of our practice, capturing sentimental, monumental, and hysterical moments."

"When it comes to marketing, we've tried everything. Nothing has worked like social media. We've seen a 20 percent increase in new patients since we started using social media."

"Our biggest social media surprise has been how willing patients are to engage with us on social media if we just ask!"

"A photo posted by a patient is worth 100 times more than a photo we post of them on our own social media page."

"My practice is less than a year old so social media marketing has helped us reach more people quicker!"

"We weren't expecting that our patients would care so much about our social media, but we were wrong. We've learned that our patients actually do care to better know us as people. We're more than an dental office to them, we're friends."

"Social media has brought our team even closer together and has shown our patients what a close-knit group we are."

"We use social media to show our friendly side and to combat those 'I'm afraid of the dentist' comments out there."

In the end, you really only have one decision to make about all this: **participate** or **don't participate.**

ONE DECISION

In the end, you really only have one decision to make about all this: participate, or don't participate. The online conversation about your practice and profession is already happening. It's just time for you to participate. You're going to see that this space is actually quite welcoming and forgiving.

After you've committed to participating, you'll be able to start differentiating your practice in ways you never could before. Remember that there's no exact blueprint for the transformation you'll go through. There will be a million tiny decisions along the way, and a few bigger ones. There will be delightful and unexpected surprises, as well as painful disappointments. This journey will shift your focus, excuse you from the rat race of outdated marketing tricks, and help you concentrate on the things that truly matter for your practice's growth and your own personal job satisfaction.

Although social media marketing has been around for a few years now, frankly, if you're reading this book, you're still an early adopter. There are still very few businesses—large or small—that really understand social media marketing and leverage it effectively. And certainly there are even fewer dental practices with that vision. Congratulations. I'm proud of you, and you should be too.

ENVISION YOUR FUTURE PRACTICE

Social media makes marketing a partnership. It isn't a zero-sum game anymore. It's a win/win. We don't have to abuse people to market to them. We're not just trying to sell people stuff. People get what they want (value). Your practice gets what it wants (growth).

Here's another cool thing we really didn't talk about much. New marketing helps you realize that, in your quest for new patients, you don't have to target every single human with teeth. Practices have been conditioned by decades of traditional marketing to believe that. Social media marketing flips that idea on its head. What if, instead of advertising to 1,000 prospective new patients and having three of them convert, we reach ten of the "right" prospective new patients and three of them convert? To reach that 1,000, we had to do a lot of things we'd rather not do. We had to try to please everyone, anyone; in the process, we delighted no one. What a relief it is to realize you can let go of that idea.

Instead, you're going to simply focus on the things that make people want what you provide. Things that make people seek you out. Things that advocates share with their trusted, permission-based and highly scalable networks. When you tell your practice story, word spreads. Prospective new patients see that yours is the kind of practice they need and want. It's simpler and a lot less stressful. Plus, you sleep better at night because you don't feel like a used car salesman.

Envision your future practice -

through the lens of new marketing.

Yes, in the beginning, social media marketing is kinda scary. It doesn't always work the way you want it to work. Start small. Take small risks first—but take them! You'll learn, and quickly get better at it. Give. Provide value. Be generous when it is easier to be selfish. Your future practice is worth it.

There are lots of ways to envision that future practice. You can think about new technologies, new treatments and new materials. You can think about new equipment and new locations. You can think about new employees or new clinical associates. They are all important considerations. But I want to challenge you, FIRST, to envision your future practice through the lens of new marketing. Doing so can have a greater impact on your practice, your lifestyle and your psyche than all of those other things combined. Grasp these opportunities. Be the practice that "gets it." Trust your gut. Focus on the believers. Over time, you'll be able to ignore the nonbelievers as you truly transform and grow the flourishing practice you desire.

You can do this. I see hundreds of practices do it every year. Onward!